# ANG ISTORYA SANG MGA NUMERO

## THE NUMBER STORY

### SMALL BOOK ONE

ENGLISH - HILIGAYNON

*Numbers Teach Children
Their Number Names*

written and illustrated by

# MISS ANNA

Early Reader Edition of *The Number Story 1*
Bronze Medal Winner, 2016 Wishing Shelf Book Award

Library of Congress Control Number: 2018902040

Names: Miss Anna, author.
Title: Number story : numbers teach children their number names / Miss Anna.
Description: Portland, OR: Lumpy Publishing, 2018.
Identifiers: ISBN 978-1-945977-67-1 | LCCN 2018902040
Summary: The pictures and rhymes present stories which introduce numbers 0-10.
Subjects: LCSH Numeration—English--Hiligaynon--Pictorial works--Juvenile literature. | BISAC JUVENILE NONFICTION /
Languages: English--Hiligaynon
Classification: LCC QA141.3 .M57 2018 | DDC 513—dc23

Publisher: Lumpy Publishing
Website: www.missannabooks.com
Email: missanna@missannabooks.com

Paperback: ISBN 978-1-945977-67-1
Printed in the U.S.A.    1 3 5 7 9 10 8 6 4 2

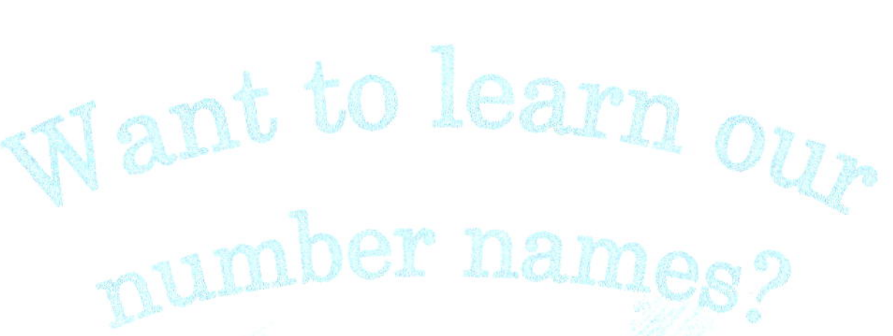

Gusto mo mabal-an ang
mga pangalan sang numero?

It is very easy and a lot of fun!

Mahapos kag masadya!

Say-along our little jingle

Kanta upod sa amon!

starting from Number One!

Masugod kita sa numero isa!

# 1

ONE looks like my one finger.

ISA

pareho sa akon isa ka tudlo.

ONE!

ISA!

# 2

TWO   trails a tail.

## DUA

May ara siya ikog.

A TAIL! IROG!

3

THREE   has bumps.

TATLO

ay isa ka daw bungsod.

Tan-awa ang mga berde na bungsod!

# 4

FOUR carries a sail.

APAT

ay isa ka baroto.

Baroto na
may layag!

# 5

FIVE   is a racing track.

LIMA

ay isa kapangkarera na aliagian.

VROOM
BRUUUM!
1

# 6

SIX curves like a snail.

## ANOM

gatiko pareho sang taklung.

A SNAIL! TAKLUNG!

7

SEVEN has a sharp angle.

PITO

May matalom na anggulo.

BE CAREFUL! IT'S SHARP!
Halong! Matalom!

8

EIGHT   is rollercoaster rails.

WALO

ay isa siya ka riles sang

"rollercoaster"

YIPPEE!
YIPPEE!

NINE   is a bubble on a stick.

SIYAM

ay isa ka bula^ sa palito.

A BUBBLE!  BULA^!

# 10

KINDAT!
WINK!

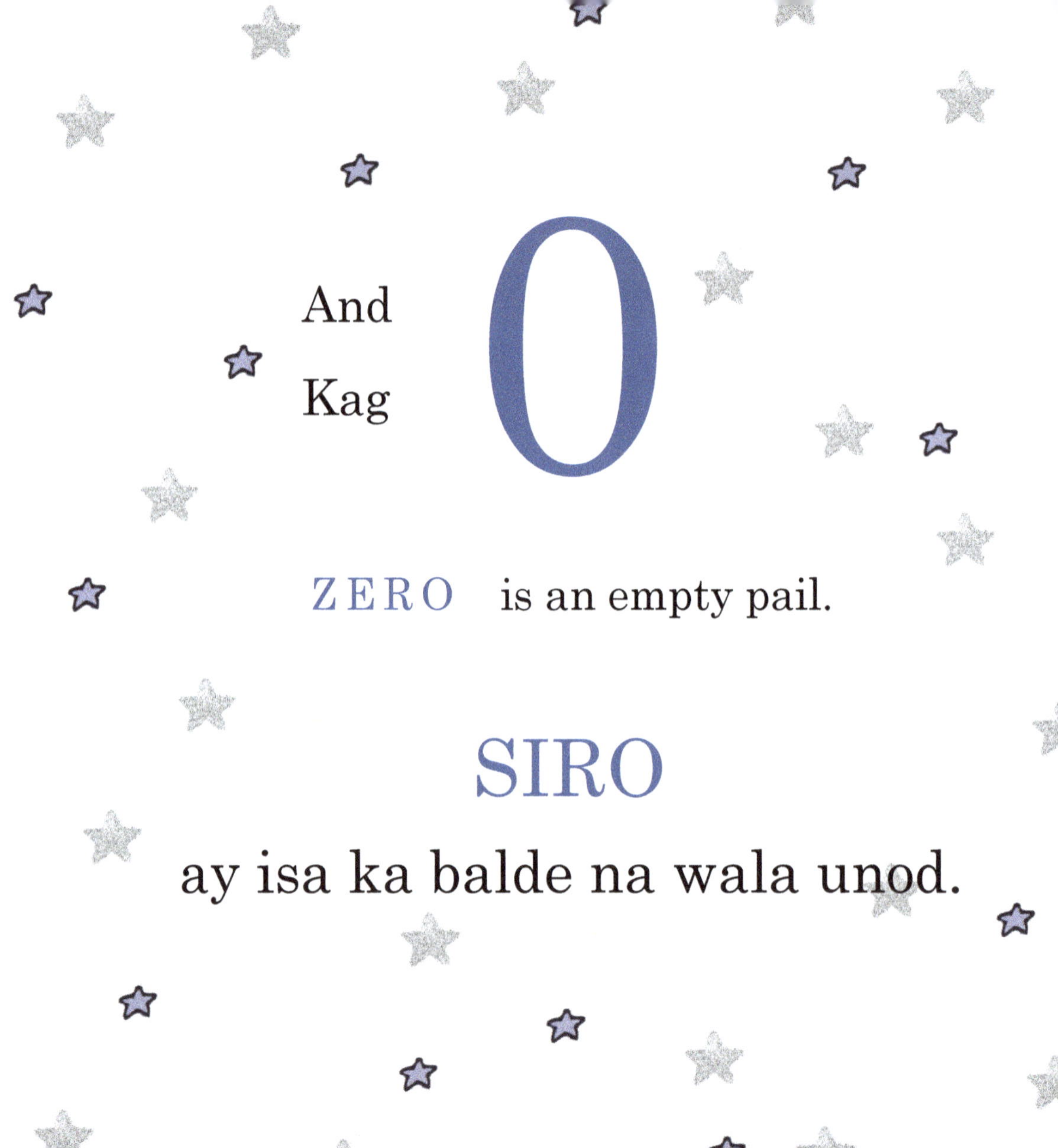

And Kag

# 0

ZERO is an empty pail.

SIRO

ay isa ka balde na wala unod.

IT'S
EMPTY!
WALA
UNOD!

Thank you for playing with us today.

We had a lot of fun too!

Salamat sa pag upod sa amon hampang subong na adlaw.

Masadya man kami!

We are your Number friends,
Zero to Ten,
Who will be here for you~
Mga migo kag miga mo kami
Siro hasta Pulo^ .
Ari kmi diri pirme para sa imo~


Bye-bye now!
See you again soon!
Bay-bay na sa subong!
Kitaay kita liwat sa dason!

The Numbers are *SINGING* too!

To sing-a-long, look for Miss Anna Number Story
at your favorite music store like iTUNES.

MP3

Numbers 0-10
IDENTIFYING
& COUNTING

Numbers 11-20
& Ordinals

first, second, third...

Numbers 0-100
& Place Values

ones, tens, hundreds...

About Clocks
& Telling Time

hours, minutes, seconds...

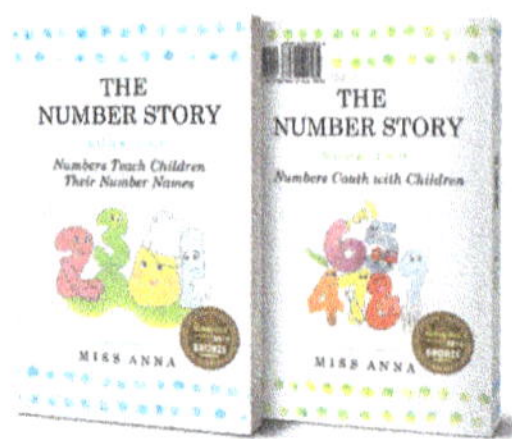

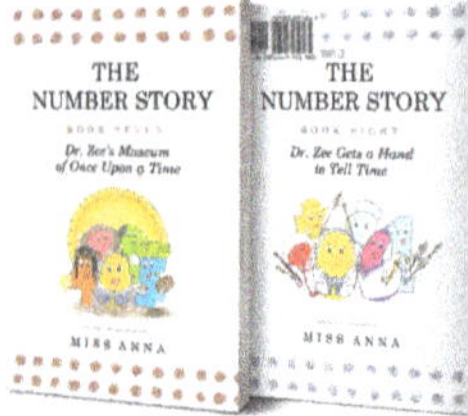

Number Story 1 & 2
isbn: 978-0-996216-48-7

Number Story 3 & 4
isbn: 978-1-945977-01-5

Number Story 5 & 6
isbn: 978-1-945977-06-0

Number Story 7 & 8
isbn: 978-1-949320-40-4

For more Miss Anna books to love,
visit us at

w w w . m i s s a n n a b o o k s . c o m

Numbers are working hard all over the world!
*Come Travel the World with Us!*